# INTRODUCTION

It is called soccer in America, fussball in Germany and voetball in Holland. In Spain it is known as futbol and in Italy they go down to the park for a game of calcio. Played in virtually every country in every continent of the world, football is the most popular game in the world.

# GUIDE TO SYMBOLS & ARROWS

To help understand movement and direction the following arrows and diagrams have been used:

The red colour burst clearly demonstrates ball and body contact.

The orange colouring shows you the foot's point of contact with the ball.

The yellow arrow indicates the action of the body.

The red arrow indicates the direction of the ball.

The diagrams further clarify the action of the drill.

# BASIC CONTROL

Keeping possession and preventing the opposition from taking control of the ball is the name of the game. That is why it is crucial for you to control it. If you have possession, it is much harder for your opponent to get it back from you and much easier for you to pass it to a teammate or shoot for goal.

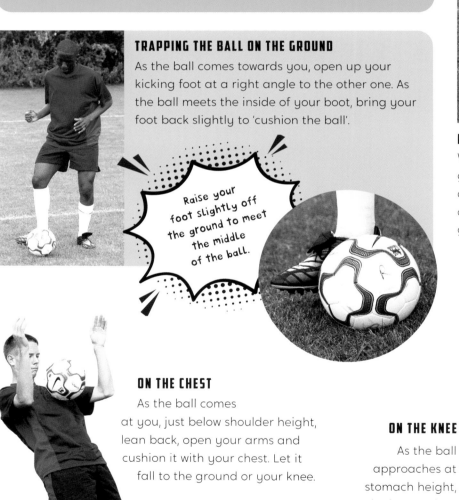

### TRAPPING THE BALL ON THE GROUND

As the ball comes towards you, open up your kicking foot at a right angle to the other one. As the ball meets the inside of your boot, bring your foot back slightly to 'cushion the ball'.

Raise your foot slightly off the ground to meet the middle of the ball.

### IN THE AIR

When the ball bounces off the ground, get your body into position and raise your foot to meet it in the air. Cushion the ball and let it drop gently to your feet.

### ON THE CHEST

As the ball comes at you, just below shoulder height, lean back, open your arms and cushion it with your chest. Let it fall to the ground or your knee.

The faster the ball is moving the farther back you must lean.

### ON THE KNEE

As the ball approaches at stomach height, let it come into your body. As it nears the stomach raise your thigh to form a platform to cushion the ball, then let it drop to your feet.

# BE THE BEST AT
# FOOTBALL

JOHN ALLAN

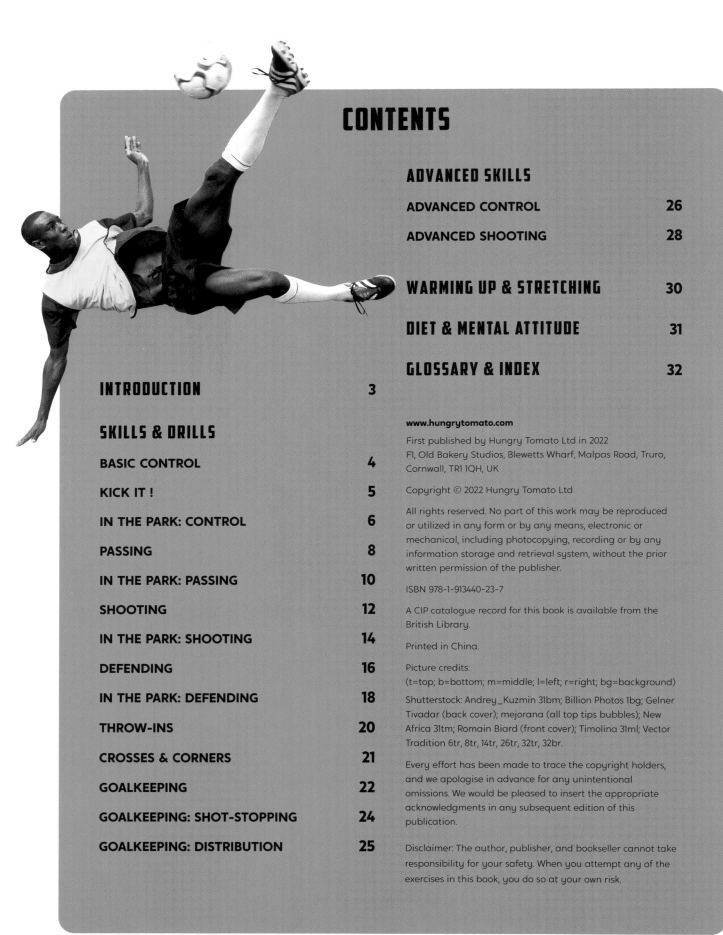

# CONTENTS

www.hungrytomato.com

First published by Hungry Tomato Ltd in 2022

F1, Old Bakery Studios, Blewetts Wharf, Malpas Road, Truro, Cornwall, TR1 1QH, UK

Copyright © 2022 Hungry Tomato Ltd

ISBN 978-1-913440-23-7

A CIP catalogue record for this book is available from the British Library.

Printed in China.

Picture credits:
(t=top; b=bottom; m=middle; l=left; r=right; bg=background)

Shutterstock: Andrey_Kuzmin 31bm; Billion Photos 1bg; Gelner Tivadar (back cover); mejorana (all top tips bubbles); New Africa 31tm; Romain Biard (front cover); Timolina 31ml; Vector Tradition 6tr, 8tr, 14tr, 26tr, 32tr, 32br.

Every effort has been made to trace the copyright holders, and we apologise in advance for any unintentional omissions. We would be pleased to insert the appropriate acknowledgments in any subsequent edition of this publication.

Disclaimer: The author, publisher, and bookseller cannot take responsibility for your safety. When you attempt any of the exercises in this book, you do so at your own risk.

## KICK IT!

**Now you've got the ball under control, use these four basic kicking skills to pass it on to a teammate.**

### THE SIDEFOOT

Bring your leg across slightly and sidefoot the ball with a short, sharp action, punching the ball hard and fast along the ground.

### STRAIGHT-ON VOLLEY

Approach the ball head-on using greater back-lift from your kicking leg. Kick it straight out in front of you, meeting the ball with the front of your foot, on the laces.

### THE DRIVE

The drive hits the ball long and into the air. Approach the ball from behind, swinging your leg back to get the power. Contact is made at the bottom of the ball to scoop it up into the air while keeping it low.

### THE SIDEFOOT VOLLEY

To accurately pass a ball in the air to a teammate, get into position as if to trap the ball in the air. Do not cushion the ball but play your foot towards it to make contact and redirect it.

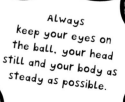

Always keep your eyes on the ball, your head still and your body as steady as possible.

# IN THE PARK: CONTROL

Here are three great drills to practice in the park to improve your ball control and balance. Try them either by yourself or with friends.

### KEEPY UPPY (1 PLAYER OR MORE)

Playing keepy uppy in the park is a great way to improve your basic ball skills. Keep the ball off the ground, counting how many times you touch the ball before you lose control – then try to keep beating your record!

### STEP 1

Try to play the ball with the front part of your foot, gently kicking the ball upwards.

### STEP 2

This will put backspin on the ball keeping it close to your foot. Also, try to use both feet, not just your strongest one.

### STEP 3

You can play the ball with both feet, your knees, chest and even your head.

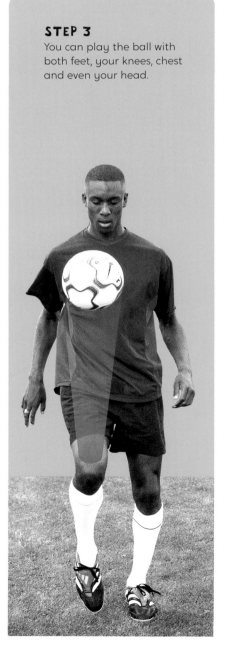

## TRAPPING CIRCLE (2-6 PLAYERS)

Stand in a circle, with each player a few metres apart. Then pass the ball to one another across the circle. Each player must control the ball with one touch, then pass it on.

## CONTROL & VOLLEY (2 PLAYERS)

This drill will help you to control balls that come to you at an awkward height.

### STEP 1

Two players stand a few yards apart. Player One then throws it gently to the other player, aiming anywhere between shoulder and knee height.

### STEP 2

Player Two must control the ball, either with the foot, knee or chest, and volley it gently back.

## TOP TIP

If you feel yourself losing control, spread your arms out to help you regain your balance.

# PASSING

Football is a team game, so it is important that once you have control of the ball you can pass it on to your teammates.

## SIDEFOOT PASSING

Using the inside of the foot is the most accurate way of passing the ball to a teammate. As it travels along the ground, it is easier to control when received.

**STEP 1**

Step up to the ball with your non-kicking leg facing in the direction you want the ball to go and bring your kicking leg back.

**STEP 2**

Keep your eyes down and your head over the ball as you bring your kicking leg forward to meet the centre of the ball with the side of your foot.

**STEP 3**

Keep your head and body steady as you follow through. The power of the kick determines the distance it travels.

## SIDEFOOT VOLLEYING

If the ball is off the ground, it is sometimes better to pass it on with a sidefoot volley than trying to control it and giving your opponents a chance to close in on you.

**STEP 1**
Steady yourself and meet the middle of the ball with the side of your foot.

**STEP 2**
Keeping your head down and your eyes on the ball, aim and follow through.

## STEP 1

Because you need more power, you will need to take a step or two back before playing the ball. Spread your arms to give you balance and step forward as you swing your kicking leg right back.

## STEP 2

Lean back very slightly as you strike the bottom of the ball with the front of your foot.

## LONG PASSING

To pass the ball over longer distances, you will need to use more power and get the ball in the air. It is not as easy to be accurate, but a perfect long pass to a teammate can give them an advantage over the opposition's defence.

## STEP 3

Keep your head down and follow through with your kicking leg.

## TOP TIP

It is always easier to play the ball in the direction you are facing so, where possible, turn to face the player before passing.

# IN THE PARK: PASSING

**Even if you have learnt the basic skills of passing, it is still important to keep practicing. Pro players regularly use the drills featured here during training to sharpen their skills.**

### PASSING SQUARE (5 PLAYERS)

**A great drill for improving passing and ball control.**

Four players stand in a square and one (Player X) in the centre. The ball is played to Player X, who traps it, turns 90 degrees to his or her right (or left) and passes it to the next player in the square. That player controls it and plays it back to the centre, where Player X controls it, turns 90 degrees and plays it to the next player. Swap around so that everyone has a go in the middle.

### 3-PLAYER PASSING DRILL

**This drill enables you to play a long pass into the path of a teammate on the run.**

Three players line up in a straight line, 5 metres (16 feet) apart. Player B, in the centre, plays the ball to Player A. As they do so, Player C sprints forward. Player A must control the ball, look up and play a long pass into the path of Player C.

## LONG PASSING DRILL (2 PLAYERS)

**This simple exercise will improve the accuracy of your long passing.**

Two players stand opposite each other, starting at about 10 metres (33 feet) apart, then gradually moving farther apart. Play long passes to one another, lifting the ball in the air aiming to place it at the feet.

## PIGGY IN THE MIDDLE (4–10 PLAYERS)

**Piggy in the middle is great for getting you used to passing under pressure.**

All the players stand in a circle (the more players involved, the bigger the circle should be), except for one who stands in the middle (Player X). The players around the circle must pass the ball to each other while Player X tries to intercept. If Player X touches the ball, the player who passed it must swap places and go in the middle. Start off allowing each player one touch to control the ball before passing it, but then insist on one-touch passing.

## TOP TIP

If you have more than eight players in the circle, place two players in the middle.

# SHOOTING

You can't win a football match without scoring goals, so shooting for goal is crucial. Much of the art of goal scoring is instinct, reacting to a situation in an instant, but by perfecting your shooting technique, you can increase your chances of success.

## SIDEFOOT SHOOTING

Sidefoot shooting is for accuracy, when you've got the space to line up a shot and go for the corner.

**STEP 1**
Keep the ball position in mind as you line up to shoot.

**STEP 2**
Make contact with the inside of your foot, angling your body.

**STEP 3**
Bring your head and upper body forward as you make good, firm contact with the middle of the ball.

## LONG-RANGE SHOOTING

To shoot from long range – anywhere outside the penalty area – you will need more power and height in your shot.

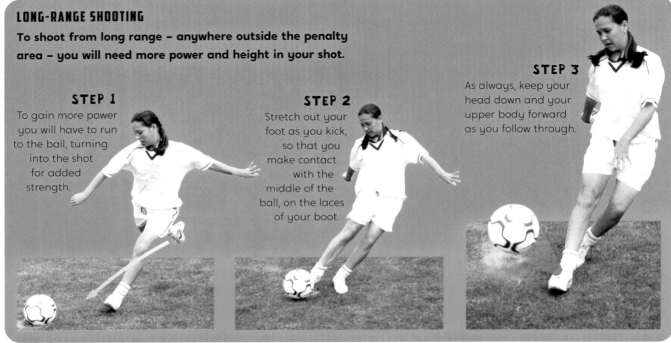

**STEP 1**
To gain more power you will have to run to the ball, turning into the shot for added strength.

**STEP 2**
Stretch out your foot as you kick, so that you make contact with the middle of the ball, on the laces of your boot.

**STEP 3**
As always, keep your head down and your upper body forward as you follow through.

## VOLLEYING

Volleying is a difficult skill to perfect. It is very difficult to time your kick so that you connect cleanly with a moving ball – but if and when you do it can be a lethal shot.

### STEP 1
As the ball comes towards you in the air, spread your arms for balance and get your body into position early.

Keep your balance with your arms and non-kicking leg as you follow through.

### STEP 2
Anticipate the pace and direction of the ball, twisting your body as you bring your kicking leg round to meet it.

Make contact with your boot laces and the middle of the ball.

## CHIPPING

Chipping is another clever skill to use if the keeper is off the goal line.

### STEP 1
You do not need much of a run-up for a chip shot as you will require a delicate touch rather than power.

### STEP 2
Keep your head down and your body back. Approach the ball at an angle, plant your non-kicking foot alongside it.

### STEP 3
To give the ball lift, you will have to make contact with the bottom centre of the ball, scooping it up into the air. On contact, stop the kicking motion. The stabbing effect should put backspin on the ball, lifting it into the air.

## TOP TIP

If you want the ball to go to your left in long-range shooting, then hit it slightly on the right, and vice versa. If you hit the ball nearer the bottom, it will go higher and travel further.

# IN THE PARK: SHOOTING

Shooting is all about making the right decision on how and where to hit the ball. These drills are designed to help you get used to first-time shooting and hitting the ball on target every time.

### TARGET PRACTICE (3–12 PLAYERS)

It is all very well getting the ball on target, but you've got a much better chance of scoring if you can hit the ball low and hard into the corner of the goal.

Place two cones or similar in a full-size goal, guarded by a goalkeeper. The server, Player X, then stands on the edge of the penalty area. The other players stand outside the box and, one by one, pass the ball to the server. Player X plays it first time (with one touch) into the box for them to run on to and shoot, aiming for one of the gaps between the post and cone.

## TOP TIP
Use the sidefoot shot in this exercise to give you the accuracy you need to hit a small gap.

## LAY-OFF SHOOTING (3-12 PLAYERS)

This drill is great for developing shooting skills around the edge of the box, but it also trains players to react quickly to a pass from a team-mate before striking.

### STEP 1
The server, Player X, stands on the edge of the penalty area. The other players line up back towards the halfway line. One by one, they play the ball into the server and run forward.

### STEP 2
The server lays the ball off into the player's path.

### STEP 3
The player must adjust instantly to the lay-off and shoot first time at the goal which is guarded by a goalkeeper.

### VARIATION
Rather than laying the ball off, the server holds the ball and bounces it into the player's path, meaning that he has to volley the ball towards the goal.

# DEFENDING

**Defenders might not get the glory, but a last-ditch tackle or goal-line clearance can be just as important in winning a match as a spectacular goal.**

## BLOCK TACKLE

**Pulling off a successful block tackle requires strength and balance as well as guts!**

*Focus on the ball. You must be sure you can win it if you're going to go for the tackle.*

### STEP 1
Get your body sideways on to your opponent and wait for the moment to pounce. When you can see that your opponent has lost control for a split-second or shown you too much of the ball, make a move.

### STEP 2
Go into the tackle leaning forward over the ball so that your body weight supports your leg. Make contact with the ball with the side of your foot.

## THE SLIDE TACKLE
**The slide tackle is a tactic that requires split-second timing and great athleticism to pull off successfully.**

### STEP 1
Watch the movement of the ball closely as you run alongside your opponent. If you think you can clear the ball, launch yourself across your opponent towards the ball.

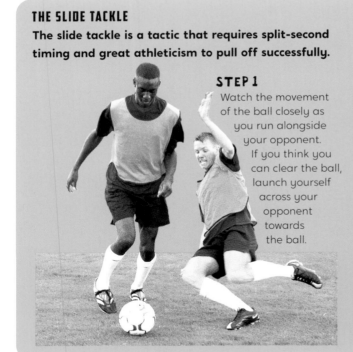

### STEP 2
Extend your kicking leg and, as you slide across your opponent's path, hook the ball away.

## INTERCEPTING

**A sharp-witted defender will be able to run in and steal the ball from right under an opposing striker's nose.**

### STEP 1

Stick close to the shoulder of the attacker you are marking, but always keep on your toes, reading the play. If a chance to intercept the ball arrives, you are ready to pounce.

### STEP 2

The ball is played in to the attacker's feet. If he is slow to move or the ball is under-hit, you have time to step in front of him and steal it.

Do not attempt to intercept if you are not certain of winning the ball.

## JOCKEYING

**Sometimes as a defender it is too risky to try to win the ball. If your opponent has it under control, the best tactic can often be to jockey, to hold them up.**

### STEP 1

Position yourself in front of your opponent. You should block the route to goal with your body, forcing your opponent wide.

### STEP 2

Continue to drop back, leaving the same gap between yourself and your opponent. Remain on your toes at all times, ready to switch sides or make a tackle if your opponent tries to get past you. Don't stand too close, or a clever opponent will be able to push the ball round you and get past.

# IN THE PARK: DEFENDING

The following drills are designed to recreate defensive situations so that defenders can practice their technique.

### JOCKEYING DRILL (2 PLAYERS)

**This drill allows defenders to practice jockeying, encouraging them not to dive in and make ill-judged tackles.**

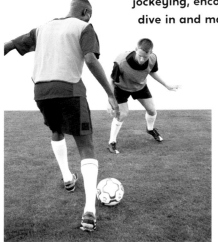

Mark out an area roughly 20 metres (60 feet) long and 4 metres (13 feet) wide. Within this area, mark out three gaps of 3 metres (10 feet) across, as shown in the diagram opposite. An attacking player is given the ball at one end of the area, and must pass through the centre of all the marker cones to the end. The defensive player jockeys him all the way, staying 'goal-side', but he must not tackle at any point. It is the defender's aim to force the attacker to play outside the cones.

### SLIDE CONE

**In training it is not always sensible to practice tackling, because players can get injured if one is mistimed. This is a non-contact drill, however, and so carries less risk of injury.**

### STEPS 1, 2, 3

The player must slide-tackle the ball without touching the cone.

## INTERCEPTION DRILL (3 PLAYERS)

**By making drills like this competitive, you add an extra dimension to training.**

Mark out an area of 7 x 7 metres (23 x 23 feet). An attacking player and a defensive player stand within this area, with the defensive player marking the attacker and the attacker trying to lose the marker. Another player stands on the edge of this box and must play the ball into the attacker's feet. The defensive player must try to intercept the ball. Whenever the attacking player collects the ball they win a point; whenever the defending player gets a touch before the opponent they win a point. The first to 10 points wins.

# THROW-INS

It is always important to keep possession for your team at a throw-in, which means the delivery must be right.

## SHORT THROW

With all throws the ball must be held in both hands. It must go fully back behind the thrower's head and be released in one fluid movement above the head, while both feet are on the ground behind the touchline.

**STEP 3**
Release the ball when it is directly over your head and follow through.

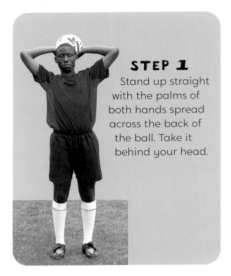

**STEP 1**
Stand up straight with the palms of both hands spread across the back of the ball. Take it behind your head.

**STEP 2**
Without moving the wrists and elbows, arch your back behind you and then quickly bring the ball forward.

## LONG THROW

To get distance and power on a throw-in, you will need to take a run-up and put your back into it.

**STEP 1**
Having taken a couple of steps back from the line, grasp the ball firmly (with both palms across the back of it).

**STEP 2**
Begin to step forward. As you do, bring the ball back behind you and step up to the line.

**STEP 3**
Plant your leading leg firmly into the ground and, as you take the ball behind your head, arch your back.

**STEP 4**
In a steady and powerful motion, use your shoulders and arms to propel the ball over your head.

## CROSSING

During a match it is quite rare to get into a good position to cross the ball, so when it happens make sure its a ball the opposition will struggle to defend.

# CROSSES & CORNERS

**People talk about great finishing, but often the greater skill is in providing the ball that has created the chance to score.**

**STEP 1**
Approach the ball from an angle. If you are right-footed, approach it from the right, and vice versa.

**STEP 2**
Spread your arms for balance and plant your non-kicking leg behind the ball.

**STEP 3**
Aim to make contact with the side of the ball. With this point of contact, and the angle of your run and follow through, your kick should curve the ball away from the keeper.

## TAKING INSWINGING CORNERS

**By swinging the ball into the goal, you put the goalkeeper under immense pressure under his own crossbar.**

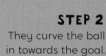

**STEP 1**
A right-footed player takes it from the left while a left-footed player takes it from the right.

**STEP 2**
They curve the ball in towards the goal.

## TAKING OUTSWINGING CORNERS

**Swinging the ball away from the goal makes it risky for the goalkeeper to intercept, but perfect for an attacking player to score.**

**STEP 1**
Taking corners incorporates all the above crossing skills.

**STEP 2**
A left-footed player should take a left-hand corner and a right-footed player should take one from the right.

# GOALKEEPING

One awesome save and the goalkeeper is the hero. Much of the art of goalkeeping, however, is about good positioning and ball handling. If a keeper has these, often a spectacular save is not needed. There is no point being able to make incredible saves if you drop the ball every time you are called upon to make a simple stop or catch.

## GATHERING THE BALL

Shots into the chest should be gathered into the stomach. If you stand up straight, the ball could easily bounce back out.

### STEP 1

Allow your body to absorb the shot by bending over and gathering the ball in.

### STEP 2

Once the ball has come into your stomach, gather your hands around it so it can't escape.

## BASIC CATCHING

When catching a ball at head height, it is vital to get your hands behind the ball, no matter how simple the catch may appear. It is these simple catches that can slip through a goalkeeper's hands due to a lack of concentration, so never think a catch is made until the ball is safely in your hands.

## LOW STOP

There is nothing worse for a goalkeeper than letting a shot slip through their legs, so make sure it doesn't happen.

Go down on one knee, using your knee as a second line of defence should the ball slip through your hands. Your legs should form a 'K' shape. Then gather the ball into your body.

## PUNCHING

If the penalty area is crowded with players, you may not be able to get a clear enough run at the ball to catch it, so you may have to punch.

### ONE-HANDED

One-handed punches are required when you need to reach over a crowd of players to clear a ball you can't catch. Clench your fist and extend your arm to its fullest point to literally punch the ball clear.

### TWO-HANDED

The secret of a good punch is to make solid contact so you get as much distance as possible. Using two hands will give you a greater chance of making good contact. Clench your fists, hold them together and punch the ball at the highest point that you can reach it.

## HIGH CATCHING

It is important to catch crosses and high balls coming into the box at the highest point possible.

**STEP 1**
Take a two or three step run-up to enable you to launch yourself into your jump.

**STEP 2**
As you launch yourself into the air, begin to extend your arms as you anticipate the movement of the ball.

**STEP 3**
Catch the ball and hold on tight. Be prepared for a bumpy landing, gathering the ball into your body as you fall.

# GOALKEEPING: SHOT-STOPPING

Good goalkeeping is about getting the simple things right, such as catches and saving. But a goalkeeper may need a little extra skill to pull off fingertip or diving saves.

### DIVING SAVE

Shot-stopping is often a matter of instinct. It is particularly important to hold on to the ball after making a save or, if that's not possible, to push it out of play or away from the danger zone.

### STEP 1
As the shot comes in, shift your bodyweight to the side the ball is approaching. Position your hands early, ready to stop it.

### STEP 2
Spread your hands so that your lower hand will stop the ball and your upper hand will come down on top of it to prevent it bouncing straight back.

### STEP 3
Bring your body down behind the ball as an extra line of defence, gathering it into your chest as you drop down on top of it.

# DISTRIBUTION

A goalkeeper who has good distribution skills can add a whole new dimension to the team, instantly turning defence into attack with a well-directed kick or throw.

## HIGH THROW

Good for accurate longer balls.

### STEP 1

Lean back and twist your arm so that the ball is held above instead of below your wrist. Keep your arm straight as you bring your upper body forward and aim.

### STEP 2

The further you need to throw it, the earlier you should release the ball. Follow through to exert maximum power and direction.

## LOW THROW

**For accurate short balls to a player's feet.**

Swing your arm forward and go down on to one knee so that, as you release the ball, it rolls smoothly along the ground. This will make it easier for the player receiving the ball to control it.

## PUNT

For less accurate but long-distance distribution.

### STEP 1

Hold the ball, cupped in both hands, ahead of you and concentrate on it. Take a two or three step run-up and release the ball, swinging your kicking leg back as you do so.

### STEP 2

Focus on the ball as you kick it, aiming to get right under the ball to lift it into the air and across the pitch.

# ADVANCED CONTROL

Once you have mastered the basics of football, you can start to be more adventurous. Instead of looking for the easy pass, you can test your skills to the maximum.

## DRIBBLING

Running with the ball under control at speed and beating players can unlock the tightest of defences.

### STEP 1

The secret of good dribbling is to keep the ball close to your feet at all times. As you run with the ball, drop your shoulder and swerve your upper body. This will confuse the defender, or defenders, in front of you.

### STEP 2

Move the ball from one foot to the other, keeping it as close to you as possible. If you can, use your body swerve and foot skills to wrong-foot an opponent and get past him.

## THE BACKHEEL

The backheel is not a difficult skill to master: the secret is being aware enough of the space and movement of your teammates behind you to make it work.

### STEP 1

As you move with the ball and are aware that a teammate is moving into the space behind you, simply move your kicking leg over the ball.

### STEP 2

Kick backwards with your heel, making good firm contact with the middle of the ball.

## CRUYFF TURN

The Cruyff turn – named after the great Dutch player of the seventies, Johan Cruyff – is a good way of finding space when you are closely marked. The trick relies on the art of surprise to buy you some time.

**STEP 1**
Moving forward with the ball, stretch out your arms and lift your kicking foot as if you are about to kick the ball.

**STEP 2**
Instead, step over the ball with your kicking leg.

**STEP 3**
Twist your body back in the direction in which you came and, at the same time, flick the ball back with the inside of your foot.

**STEP 4**
Complete the 180 degree turn and move away with the ball.

## THE STEP-OVER

The step-over is a great trick to use to get past a player.

**STEP 1**
As you meet a defender, move your kicking foot inside the ball as if you are going to flick it round him with the outside of your boot.

**STEP 2**
Instead of flicking the ball with your kicking foot, step over it. Hopefully this will confuse your opponent.

**STEP 3**
Shift your body weight the other way and flick the ball with your other foot to out maneuver a defender.

**STEP 4**
Run past the defender on the other side. Hopefully he will have been fooled by your trick.

# ADVANCED SHOOTING

It is very rare to get an easy shooting chance in football, and sometimes you have to do something quite special to score a goal.

## OVERHEAD KICK

This is the one of the hardest football skills to execute, but when it comes off it can be truly spectacular.

## STEP 1

You can only attempt an overhead kick if the ball is coming across you in the air when you have your back to goal. If you think an overhead kick is needed, anticipate the flight of the ball, begin to lean back and shift your weight onto your kicking leg.

## STEP 2

Focus on the flight of the ball as you stretch your arms out, continue to lean back and bring your non-kicking leg up.

**WARNING:** The overhead kick is a move of extreme athleticism so be very careful when practicing it. Make sure that you land on soft grass, sand or a mat.

## STEP 3

Bring your non-kicking leg higher still, using your kicking leg for balance as the ball gets close.

## STEP 4

At the last moment spring off with your kicking leg, crossing your legs like scissors in mid-air for balance, and make contact with the ball as your body is parallel to the ground. Extend your foot towards your head so that you kick the ball over your shoulder.

## CURLING THE BALL

Curling the ball is another difficult skill. The secret is to strike through one side of the ball, putting spin on it as you follow through.

### STEP 1

Approach the ball from an angle of virtually 90 degrees. If you are right-footed the goal should be to your left, and vice versa.

### STEP 2

Shape up to the ball and strike it, aiming for the side, and make contact with the inside of your foot. This, combined with the twisting of your body towards the goal, will exert the spin that curls the ball.

## OUTSIDE OF THE BOOT

### STEP 1

Approach the ball from the opposite side to how you would if you were striking with the inside of your foot (right-footed players should have the goal to their right), but at a less severe angle. Strike the near side of the ball, with the outside of your boot.

### STEP 2

Follow through in the same way as before, keeping your body forward and your head down.

## TOP TIP

For curled shots that require height and distance, hit the ball on the side but towards the bottom. For shots that travel just off the ground strike the ball on the side, but more towards the top to keep it down.

# WARMING UP & STRETCHING

**Warming up and stretching before a training session or a match is very important. It lessens the chances of injury and increases a player's speed and ability to twist and turn.**

## WARMING UP

Before you kick a ball or even begin stretching, it is important to warm up your body. This dramatically lessens your chance of pulling a muscle or a tendon (the cause of more than half of all sports injuries). All you need to do is a light jog for five minutes. This will increase your heart rate and get the blood pumping around your body.

## STRETCHING

You must be very careful with your stretching.

- **Never stretch until the body is warmed up.**
- **Always stretch slowly and gently and never so much that it is uncomfortable.**
- **Hold each stretch for 10 to 20 seconds, keeping your body steady at all times.**
- **Never rock or bounce on a stretch.**
- **Breathe out as you stretch.**
- **Stretch both before and after exercise.**

There are many stretches, but here are some of the most important. Ask a coach or a physiotherapist to show you others, and check that you are doing them correctly.

### PELICAN THIGH STRETCH

Stand on one leg, holding the foot of your other leg behind your buttocks with your knees close together. Maintain balance and stretch.

### CALF STRETCH

Put the weight of your body on the front foot, bending the knee and stretching the other leg behind with the weight resting on your toes. Then lean forward so that your hands touch the ground, and slowly push your outstretched leg back.

### GROIN STRETCH

Sit on the ground with the soles of your feet together and your knees bent, pointing away from you. Then, using your elbows, press your knees down so that you feel a gentle stretch in the groin area.

### TWO'S COMPANY

Some stretches can be done with a teammate. This develops better balance. Keep the stretch steady and safe.

### HAMSTRING STRETCH

Kneel on the ground and stretch one leg out in front of you. Put your heel in the ground and your toe pointing in the air until you feel slight tension in the hamstring (this runs down the back of the thigh). Once the tension subsides pull your toes towards you for a further stretch.

# DIET

You can't make yourself more skillful by consuming certain foods, but you can give yourself more energy and stamina on the pitch by eating a well balanced diet.

## ENERGY BUSTERS

If you are doing a lot of exercise, then you need to eat plenty of **carbohydrates** to provide the energy for the exercise you are doing.

*Protein* is required for the growth and repair of the body, but try to choose low-fat sources, since some fatty foods can cause stomach discomfort if eaten before exercising.

## BEFORE THE MATCH

To produce the maximum energy before a match or training, you should eat *a high-carbohydrate meal at least three hours before the game.* Low-fat pasta or rice dishes (with no creamy sauce) are ideal.

In the run-up to the game, *boost your carbohydrate levels with fast-digesting snacks, such as bananas or dried fruit.*

It is crucial to *drink plenty of liquid before a game*. Water or isotonic sports drinks consumed two or three hours before playing will make up for the water you lose (through sweat) when playing.

Don't forget to stay hydrated by drinking plenty of water throughout the day!

# MENTAL ATTITUDE

As well as preparing the body, it is also important to prepare the mind for a match and even training. Much of the skill of being a good football player is to do it with confidence and self-belief. If you believe that you will score the penalty then the chances are you will.

## MIND & BODY

The strength of a football player comes from both mind and body.

It is important to do other forms of exercise to strengthen all areas of the body. Full physical fitness makes the mind more alert and decisive. Do not underestimate the level of concentration and quick-thinking that is required on the field.

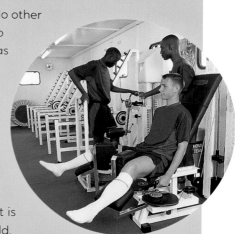

## MENTAL PREPARATION

Before a game you should focus your mind on the task ahead, visualising certain match situations and how you would deal with them in your head.

Picture yourself scoring the goal, making the spectacular save or the last-ditch tackle. Focus your mind on the game as an individual player and as a team (it is the responsibility of the captain or coach to do this). If you believe you are going to win, you probably will. You will certainly have a better chance.

# GLOSSARY

**Attacker** A player whose main objective is to score goals and create scoring chances for others.

**Backpass** A ball played backwards to a player or to his own goalkeeper.

**Chip** A lofted pass or shot.

**Corner kick** A ball kicked from the point where the touchline meets the dead-ball line after the ball has gone out of play over the dead-ball line (a defending player having touched it last).

**Defender** A player who generally plays close to his own team's goal whose main objective is to prevent the opposition from scoring.

**Foul** Any piece of play or incident on the pitch that contravenes the rules and regulations of the game.

**Goal** A point-scoring play achieved when the ball legally crosses the goal line, under the crossbar and between the posts. The word is also used for the actual structure created by posts, crossbar and a net.

**Goalkeeper** The player responsible for preventing the opposition's ball from entering the net and scoring a goal. The only player on the pitch who is allowed to use their hands to play the ball. They can move anywhere on the pitch but cannot handle the ball outside their team's penalty area.

**Lay-off** Short pass into the path of a teammate.

**Midfielder** A player who generally plays in the space between his team's attack and defence, combining the roles of attacker and defender.

**Offside** a player is considered offside if he or she receives the ball while being beyond the second last opponent (usually a defender).

**Pass** An intentional ball played to a teammate.

**Save** A play made when a goalkeeper successfully intercepts a strike on goal.

**Shot** An attempt at goal.

**Throw-in** A two-armed overhead throw from the touchline, used after the ball has gone out of play.

**Volley** A kick where the foot meets the ball in the air before it touches the ground.

**Wall** A voluntary line-up of defenders to protect their goal from a free kick. Must be at least 9.14 metres (10 yards) from the ball.

# INDEX